style

bathing

acknowledgements

I would like to thank Matt Handbury, Anne Wilson and Catie Ziller for the opportunity to work on this project and for their continued support, Anna Waddington for her endless hard work and Marylouise Brammer for her creativity, Susin Chow for making sense of the copy and everyone at Murdoch Books who was involved in this book from start to finish.

I would also like to say a big thank you to photographer Chris Craymer for his creativity, endless enthusiasm and capturing the spirit and energy of this book on film. Special thanks to make-up artist and hair stylist Dennie Pasion for your wonderful work, constant support and all the laughs when the going got tough. Special thanks to models Willa, Julie, Kirsten and baby Katie and to Camilla for getting things organised and being so calm. I would also like to thank Susie, Stewart, Nicola, Sam and Michael for their support and understanding when the pressure was on, Brenda for her inspiration and Brian for his drive. I couldn't have got this far without you all. Thank you for the loan of all the wonderful products and clothing for photography from Zarvis, Opal of London, The Bath House, Droyt's, Woodspirits UK, Jo Malone, E'SPA, Chanel, Crabtree & Evelyn, Czech & Speake, Penhaligons, Lancôme, Aveda, Perfumes Isabell, Dyptique, Aromatique, Calvin Klein, Issey Miyake, Annick Goutal, Neal's Yard Remedies, Origins, L'Occitane, Toast, Browns Living.

Special thanks to Sam Girdwood, Catie Briscoe, Nancy Brady, Trudi Collister, Anita Grossman, Suzanne Johnson at Balance, Kelly Goldenberg, the team at Karen Berman Consultancy, Astrid Sutton Associates, Riverhouse Creative Consultants, Halphern Associates, Red Rooster PR and to all the staff at Babington House.

Special thanks to Babington House, Kilmersdon, Somerset BA11 3RW, ph 44 1373 812266, for providing a wonderful setting to shoot in.

style

bathing

jane campsie

photography by chris craymer

TIME
LIFE
BOOKS

contents

cleanse

purify

refresh

the bathing ritual

revive

pamper

indulge

the history of bathing

The Egyptians were obsessed with personal hygiene, the Romans engaged in bathing as a ceremonial ritual, and for the Turks the bathhouse was a social and recreational center that was an indispensable part of daily life. For centuries, people have taken to the waters in nature's own hot springs, in opulent marble bathhouses or in open-air bath tubs. It was not until the advent of Christianity that dramatic changes occurred affecting both the social and beautifying benefits of bathing. Considered to be dangerously sensual and to have the potential for leading devout Christians astray, bathing became an act associated with licentiousness and eroticism and in many Western cultures was no longer favorable. But by the late 19th century, bathing slowly gained acceptance again when it was advised for hygienic reasons. Today, the sensual and physical pleasures of bathing are so appealing, it's essential to take time out to wallow in the tub and so improve the state of your mind, body, and spirit.

cultural rituals

japanese bathing

The Japanese get clean to bathe. Ancient traditions made scrubbing and cleansing the skin a prerequisite before soaking in the *hinokiburo*, a traditional Japanese bathtub. In comparison, the standard Western body wash is a superficial and perfunctory once-over with soap, and not worth comparing. Because Japan is situated on volcanic islands bubbling with over 20,000 hot springs, it's not surprising that bathing has become such an art form. Bathing Japanese style at the communal hot springs, or *onsens*, was a holistic experience and a time to catch up with the family and friends, scrub backs, and drink sake, whereas bathing at home, in solitude, was a time for centering, rebalancing, and recovering a sense of well-being.

roman baths

To the ancient Romans, bathing was considered both a ritual and a social affair, rather than simply a means to cleanse the body. Bathing was a communal experience that could last up to 5 hours. The famous *thermae*, or baths, were based on Egyptian precedents, and worked on the basis that bathers had to work up a sweat before being scrubbed and then soaking in hot and cold tubs.

turkish baths

When bathing Turkish style, the emphasis was on spiritual and physical rejuvenation. A few hours in the *hamman*, or bathhouse, helped to free the body of toxins, opened up the pores, cleaned the skin, and supposedly cured diarrhea, scabies, high fever, rheumatism, chronic depression, and impotence. The Turks believed that the intense heat of the *hamman* enhanced fertility and if husbands denied their wives their visits to the bathhouse, the women had grounds for divorce. Important occasions, such as a newborn's fortieth day and weddings, were always celebrated at the *hamman*. These bathing establishments were originally complementary to mosques, but today they are still used as public bathhouses.

global bathing tips

scrub up

The Japanese believe that the secret to radiant skin and a beautiful body lies in soaking in the tub and giving your skin intermittent scrubbing sessions. You don't need to splurge on fancy exfoliators — you can simply use a handful of coarse salt or a muslin bag filled with rice bran. Soak yourself for 5 minutes then scrub your body, and repeat each step three times.

floral waters

The Romans scattered rose petals on the surface of the water to condition and scent their baths. They recognized the antiseptic properties of the flower and its abundance of vitamin C. Try scattering fresh petals into your bath water and also sprinkle in a couple of drops of rose essential oil.

skin softeners

The Turks believed that working up a sweat before entering the bath helped to expel micro-nasties via the skin. You should either do some physical exercise or take a sauna before getting into a bathtub that has been laced with deep-cleansing ingredients.

To remove impurities and keep their skin and hair ultrasmooth, the Turkish women used *halawa*, a concoction of cooked sugar, honey, olive, and lemon. To create natural exfoliators and body buffers, try smoothing on a paste made from papaya, apple, grapefruit, or pineapple. All of these fruits contain enzymes that help lift off dead skin cells and improve the radiance of your skin. Simply grate the fruit, smooth over your skin, and leave for 10 minutes before rinsing with warm water.

global bathing tips

body buffing

The Scandinavians practiced head-to-toe dry skin brushing to boost circulation, remove impurities and buff the skin. It offers the same stimulation as a good massage or 20 minutes of exercise (although it shouldn't replace physical activity). With a stiff-bristled brush, start on the soles of the feet using sweeping strokes and gradually work up the legs, over the abdomen and torso, always brushing toward the heart. Glide the brush up your arms and then up your back. You should always start by applying gentle pressure; as you become used to dry skin brushing, you can exert more pressure.

brush strokes

You should always avoid brushing patches of broken skin, varicose veins, and eczema. If you have sensitive skin, you can use a cotton towel, instead of a stiff-bristled brush, to rub over your body before bathing.

Try to practice dry skin brushing daily, but make sure that you also take a week's break once every month, otherwise your skin becomes used to the treatment and dry skin brushing will be less effective.

Wash your body brush regularly using hot soapy water to remove impurities and dead skin cells, and allow the brush to dry naturally.

balance

harmony

peace

time in the tub

tranquillity

comfort

pleasure

the right ambience

Make the most of your time in the tub. Recent research shows 46 percent of women relax by taking a bath, while others brainstorm, chat on the phone, or make plans. To fully reap the benefits of bathing, be sure you create the right environment to harmonize with the way you want to feel. To relax and unwind, make sure your bathroom is softly lit (candles are preferable to electric lighting) and warm with no drafts. Avoid interruptions while you bathe — put on your answering machine or take your phone off the hook, and then listen to soothing sounds, drink chamomile tea and vaporize calming essences of lavender or jasmine oil. If you want an invigorating experience, make sure your bathroom has ample daylight (or invest in a full-spectrum light bulb, which is similar to natural sunlight — available from lighting and home-improvement stores) and is not too hot. Listen to uplifting music and vaporize energizing essences of peppermint or eucalyptus oil. After bathing, take a cold shower to jump-start the circulation.

water works

life essence

Water is the source of life. About 70 percent of an adult's body weight is water. We lose roughly 10 oz (300 ml) of water a day simply by breathing. Minor dehydration can interfere with brain power and bowel and kidney functions and triggers premature skin aging. Try to drink at least 1 qt (1 l) of water each day.

water supply

The amount of water used for baths and showers accounts for one third of the total supply used in a household each year. The average 5-minute shower uses 8 gal (30 l) of water and a bathtub, 22 gal (85 l). This is alarming when 40 percent of the world population faces water shortages.

Conserve water by turning off taps properly (one dripping faucet can waste 1,300 gal (5,000 l) of water a year) and use only the necessary amount.

temperature control

Bath water should be no hotter than 98.6°F (37°C), otherwise it increases your heart rate and leaves you feeling drained and lethargic.

handy tips

If a dirty ring appears around the tub after bathing, it could be due to hard water. Soap reacts with the salts in hard water, forming a grimy-looking mask. To remove, use a nonabrasive detergent and a bit of elbow grease. To soften hard water, sprinkle half a cup of baking soda into the water.

bathing essentials

body cleansers

Look for soap-free or pH-balanced bath bars or cleansers that work in harmony with the natural equilibrium of the skin. Cheap soaps are false economy — they won't last, can dry out the skin, and usually contain artificial lathering agents. A quality soap lathers well after a few turns in the hands.

sponges

Natural sponges are a good investment; they are gentle on the skin and help remove dead skin cells and impurities. To clean sponges, soak in vinegar overnight and rinse with warm water.

loofahs

Made from dried plants of the cucumber family, loofahs are used to buff away dead skin cells and pep up circulation. Use only on damp skin; afterward, wash the loofah thoroughly to remove traces of soap and hang it to dry, otherwise it can go moldy. Or use mitts, body scrubs, or exfoliating cloths to buff the skin.

washcloths

Suitable for the face or body, cotton washcloths should be rinsed with soap and hot water after use and laundered in the washing machine frequently.

pumice stones

Made from volcanic lava, pumice is porous and light enough to float. It has long been used to remove calluses and buildup of dead skin on the feet, hands, and body. Now terra-cotta and other natural materials are also being used to buff stubborn dead skin. Remember, overzealous scrubbing removes the skin's natural oils.

body brushes

A stiff-bristled brush is a must-have for dry skin brushing to exfoliate the skin, stimulate circulation, and help remove toxins. Before dry skin brushing, add a droplet of rose or lavender essential oil to the bristles to disinfect them. Every 7 to 10 days, wash your body brush with hot, soapy water.

bathing etiquette

DO NOT soak in the tub for more than 20 minutes at a time — extended wallowing in the bath can dry out your skin and zap your energy.

IF YOU want to relax while in the bath, fold up a hand towel or half fill a hot water bottle and use as a pillow.

ALWAYS WAIT at least 40 minutes after you've consumed a meal before taking a bath or shower.

AVOID SOAKING in a hot bubble bath if you have dry skin. The water temperature and the bubbles will dehydrate your skin.

TRY TO go to bed after a warm bath; it helps ensure a good night's sleep.

IT IS not advisable to drink alcohol in the bathtub. Alcohol dilates the blood vessels and is a stimulant that generates heat within the body. When teamed with warm water, this can cause an adverse reaction.

AFTER BATHING gently pat the skin dry with a cotton towel and slather a hydrating body lotion on to damp skin.

NEVER HAVE more than two baths or showers in one day; you could strip the skin of its essential essences.

aroma

sense

smell

fragrant bathing

mood

essence

spirit

aromatherapy baths

Aromatherapy uses the essential oils of plants to enhance physical and mental well-being. For centuries, essential oils have been used for aromatic baths, massage, scenting rooms, and as a natural cure-all. Some odoriferous molecules actually penetrate the skin to take action, while others stimulate nerve endings as they are inhaled. Whilst bathing, the steam carries more aroma molecules to the nose than when we wear fragrance or use an oil burner. It takes just two seconds for an aroma to enter the nose and travel to the part of the brain that controls our memory and emotions. Once aromatherapy oils have infused the air, they remain for approximately 15 minutes, although our noses become accustomed to the fragrance after a few minutes and then stop registering the aroma. When this happens, do not pour more oils into the bath — essential oils are potent substances and overusing them can counteract their benefits. For example, peppermint stimulates digestion, but if you use too much, it will cause nausea. Always stick to the recommended doses.

When buying essential oils, choose reputable brands. Price is usually a good indication of quality — large amounts of plant material are required to produce a small amount of oil, which makes essential oils expensive. Cheap versions are not necessarily pure, natural essences — they may contain synthetic or adulterated products that make the oils less effective.

aromatherapy essences

rose

The fresh aroma of rose is calming, balancing, and very sensual. It brings feelings of happiness and contentment and is recommended for depression, relieving symptoms of PMS, and regulating menstruation. It's a great tonic for dry and mature skins, purifies the blood, and strengthens the heart.

chamomile

This floral oil is purifying, soothing, calming, and restorative. Chamomile oil doesn't mix well with water, and when added to the bath, it tends to cling to the sides of the tub. Mixed with other oils and added to the bath, it can work wonders, relieving stress and tension. Chamomile is safe to use if pregnant.

bergamot

Extracted from the peel of the nearly ripe citrus fruit, bergamot oil is known for its uplifting, reviving, and rebalancing characteristics. Bergamot is particularly valuable for treating conditions such as anxiety, depression, stress, and fatigue, and it is responsible for the aromatic taste of Earl Grey tea.

jasmine

This oil has a warm, exotic aroma and is reputed to be balancing, euphoric, and an aphrodisiac. A whiff of jasmine instantly lifts your spirits and instills good karma. Use it for treating PMS, dry skin, stretch marks, joint pain, and dermatitis. After rose, it's the most expensive oil to produce.

neroli

Extracted from orange blossoms, neroli oil has antiseptic, antispasmodic, and uplifting properties. Neroli is also recommended as an aphrodisiac, and to treat stretch marks, anxiety, depression, and PMS.

geranium

Extracted from the leaves and flowers of the geranium plant, this fresh-smelling oil has balancing and uplifting properties and is recommended for treating dry skin, nervous tension, and infections.

aromatherapy essences

lavender

Calming, antiseptic, and in large doses stimulating, this oil improves mental clarity, and treats insomnia, headaches, fevers, and stress, as well as bites, stings, burns, and skin complaints. Lavender is one of the only oils, including tea tree, that can be applied directly to the skin.

ylang-ylang

A sweet, exotic oil that's calming, balancing, and an aphrodisiac, it is also recommended for depression, stress, and instilling harmony. Too much can cause headaches and nausea.

cedarwood

This rich, aromatic oil brings balance and harmony and is an effective cleanser. High doses can irritate the skin so never add more than two drops to the bath. Do not use while pregnant.

cinnamon

This spicy oil, used in the bath or for massage, aids respiration, circulation, and digestion. It can cause irritation, so always dilute with base oils first.

sandalwood

This rich aroma indulges the senses but it's also a powerful decongestant and effective at eliminating bacteria. Added to a bath, it's great for treating dry, dehydrated skin. Blended with a base oil and used in massage, it can ease urinary tract infections.

eucalyptus

This strong-scented oil is a powerful antiseptic and disinfectant. It works wonders clearing symptoms of colds and congestion and speeds the healing of infections and wounds. Also use it to clear the mind and refresh emotions.

rosemary

This oil has antiseptic, antibacterial, and stimulating properties ideal for treating skin problems, allergies, colds, infections, aches, and pains. Large doses can be sedating. It shouldn't be used by epileptics or during pregnancy.

You should always consult a qualified aromatherapist before using essential oils, especially if you are pregnant.

skin survival

dry skin

Often caused by changes in climate, nutritional imbalances and stress, dry skin will benefit from a concoction of two drops each of rose and sandalwood oils added to the bath. To step up the hydrating properties, add a few teaspoons of vegetable oil, such as jojoba or sweet almond oil, to the water. Drink lots of water and take capsules of evening primrose oil daily.

sensitive skin

If your skin flares up or becomes irritated after exposure to the sun, from temperature changes, or from using harsh cosmetic preparations and chemical sunscreens, soothe with a calming bath blend of chamomile and rose oils. Avoid using heavily perfumed preparations (many contain synthetic ingredients that can irritate the skin). You should also avoid contact with very hot water and avoid spicy foods.

problem skin

If your back and chest are plagued by blemishes and pimples, relax in a bath mixed with two drops each of lavender and tea tree oils, which are known for their antibacterial and calming properties. To help zap any spots, dab neat lavender or tea tree oil onto the affected area and wear cotton clothing next to the skin (synthetic fabrics can cause irritation).

normal skin

If you are fortunate to have been blessed with normal skin, look after it. Relax in a warm bath infused with one drop each of jasmine, geranium, and rose oils to help maintain the skin's natural equilibrium. Before bathing, try dry skin brushing or get to work with a loofah once in the tub to slough off dead skin cells and impurities. Always keep the skin's moisture content up with a rich hydrator.

bath blends

chill out

If you're overworked and under pressure, you'll probably have frayed nerves and may find it difficult to relax. To de-stress, wallow in a warm bath enhanced with two drops each of rose, chamomile, cedarwood, and sandalwood essential oils. To help ensure a peaceful night's sleep, try massaging the soles of your feet with coconut oil before you go to bed.

jump-start

Late nights and the fast pace of life can leave you tired and apathetic, even after a good sleep. For a jump-start in the mornings, lace bath water with a blend of two drops each of grapefruit, lemon and pine oils, and a tablespoon of vegetable oil. Or you can add the essential oils to a damp face cloth and work it over the body to pep up the circulation. Finish with a cold shower. For an instant pick-me-up throughout the day, add a drop of eucalyptus oil to a handkerchief, and when you're at a low ebb, inhale deeply.

energy boost

When your energy is low and your spirits are flagging, indulge in a revitalizing bath. Add two drops each of peppermint, geranium, and rosemary oils to the bath water to recharge your battery. Afterward, concoct a high-energy drink by mixing a banana with soy milk and honey in a blender.

body booster

If you've had a long day and ache from head to toe, take to the bathtub and soak away your aches and pains. Blend one drop each of basil, rosemary, and marjoram oils, three drops of lavender, and 2 oz (60 ml) of avocado oil and store in a brown glass bottle. Pour some of this rescue remedy into a warm bath and relax for 10 to 15 minutes. To ease aching muscles, rope someone else into giving you a massage or do some gentle stretching exercises after your bath. If you're suffering muscular pains from too much exercise, try adding five drops of rosemary oil to a warm bath.

bath blends

detox treat

Lack of exercise, convenience foods, and a sedentary but stressful lifestyle takes its toll on the body. Toxins build up, circulation becomes sluggish, and you feel lethargic. To help the body's functions get back in synch, add one drop each of eucalyptus, lemongrass, tea tree, and lavender essential oils to the bath, with a tablespoon of milk. Increase your intake of water to flush out toxins, and exercise regularly.

sensuous bath

To enhance your powers of attraction and improve the feel-good factor of bathing, add two drops each of rose, neroli, and lavender essential oils to the bath water. It leaves your skin delicately scented and makes you feel irresistible. To further heighten your sensuality, spritz your favorite fragrance on the pulse points on the inside of your wrist and in your cleavage, but never dab the fragrance behind your ears.

hangover tonic

For a morning-after pick-me-up, add three drops of juniper essential oil and two drops each of fennel and lavender essential oils to a warm bath. To help clear your head, finish bathing with a blitz of cold water under the shower. You should always drink lots of water to counteract the dehydrating effects of alcohol — and dissolve two effervescent vitamin C tablets in a large glass of water and drink.

aromatic ingredients

herbal infusions

Rather than adding aromatherapy oils or preblended essences to the bath, use infusions of fresh or dried herbs. You can sprinkle the herbs directly into the bathtub while the water is running, or make an infusion by placing the ingredients in a square of muslin or cotton fabric and tying it closed with a piece of string. The herb bag can then be attached to the faucet so it hangs under the running water.

natural additives

Herbal tea bags are an easy-to-use alternative to oils for dropping into bath water. Chamomile soothes and relaxes the mind and body, peppermint acts as a pick-me-up, jasmine lends itself to a sensual soak. Use ginseng for an energizing experience. For the best results, use two or three bags. Or you can add a couple of cinnamon sticks to the bath to spice up the water,

fresh pine sprigs to jump-start the senses in the mornings and improve your clarity of mind, or a handful of oatmeal to soothe itchy skin.

floral water

The Romans scattered rose petals in their baths, stuffed their mattresses with flowers, and sprinkled floral waters and eau de cologne over themselves and their belongings. To create your own scented waters, add fresh or dried petals to boiling water, steep for 20 minutes, strain off the liquid, and then store in a glass bottle. Splash on your body, spray on your hair, or sprinkle into the bath water. Floral waters are ideal for those who have sensitive skin. Or you can scatter a cupful of dried chamomile flowers, rose petals, and lavender into the bath; better yet, put the flowers into a muslin bag and throw the bag into the tub (it makes cleanup easier).

aromatherapy guidelines

ADD ESSENTIAL oils to the bath once the water has finished running and then agitate the bath water to evenly disperse the droplets of oil.

ONCE OILS have been absorbed into the body, via the skin, their effects remain true for between 4 to 6 hours, provided you don't consume any alcohol or caffeine.

NEVER HAVE an aromatherapy massage and then take a bath; you will wash away the skin-conditioning benefits of the oils.

ALWAYS CLOSE the bathroom door or windows before taking an aromatherapy bath, otherwise the aromatic vapors will escape.

IF YOU are pregnant, suffer from high blood pressure, epilepsy, or other medical condition, avoid aromatherapy oils unless professionally advised.

STORE ESSENTIAL oils in a dry place, away from direct sunlight in airtight, dark glass bottles and use within six months of opening.

THE HEAT of the water increases the oil's ability to penetrate the skin so don't be heavy-handed when you're adding oils to a hot bath.

IT IS safe to use many undiluted oils in bath water, but if you have very sensitive skin, dilute with a tablespoon of milk. The milk helps the oil mix with the water and allows for better skin

splash

spray

immerse

water therapies

soak

sprinkle

shower

aqua tonic

hydrotherapy

This type of treatment uses water, usually from a mineral spring, to relieve everything from aches and pains, stress and skin disorders to sports injuries. For maximum benefit, water temperatures are alternated. Hot water is initially used to stimulate and has a secondary relaxing effect, and cold water invigorates and tones. The greater the difference in temperature, the greater the effects. Water therapies became popular during the 19th century when a Catholic priest, Sebastian Kneipp, recovered from tuberculosis after being treated with various water therapies. He went on to develop more than 100 different healing methods, and these are still practiced at health spas worldwide.

thalassotherapy

From the Greek *thalassa*, meaning sea, this uses sea water and marine extracts in a variety of different treatments to alleviate stress, tension, allergies, arthritis, and rheumatism. The minerals and trace elements found in sea water are similar to those of blood plasma, and the body is able to absorb these minerals from water therapies via the skin, especially when water is heated to body temperature. Seaweed is a vital element in thalassotherapy. It's a rich source of iodine, a mineral that stimulates the thyroid gland to produce the hormone thyroxine, the primary regulator of the body's metabolism. Incorporated into treatments, seaweed is reputed to boost circulation, eliminate toxins, and relieve fatigue.

water treatments

body blitz

To stimulate blood flow, hydrotherapy centers use high-powered water jets to target problem areas of the body, alternating the water temperature from hot to cold. For at home body blitzing, start with a warm shower, switch to cold water for about 20 seconds, then back to warm for 1 to 2 minutes and finish with a blast of cold. This is an ideal way to build resistance to minor ills and revitalize the complexion. To target problem areas on the hips and thighs, work over the skin in circular motions with the shower nozzle, holding it approximately 4 in (10 cm) from the body, alternating the water temperature from warm to cold several times for maximum benefit.

epsom salts bath

For soothing general aches and pains and flushing toxins from your body, try adding 2 cups of Epsom salts (available from pharmacies) to a hot bath. Soak in the bathtub for 20 minutes, adding more hot water as necessary to maintain a constant temperature. Afterward, dry off quickly and get into a preheated bed. Expect to sweat profusely and sleep deeply, and don't be alarmed — this is simply part of the purification process. Have a large glass of water by your bed as it's likely you will wake up thirsty. This type of salt bath is not recommended for those with eczema or high blood pressure, or for those who are pregnant.

water treatments

sitz bath

Popular in Germany and Austria, sitz baths improve circulation, help with digestive problems and enhance relaxation. The lower part of the body is submerged in hot and then cold water.

The change in water temperatures rapidly steps up circulation and flushes the lower body with oxygenated blood, removing stagnant fluids fast. For a do-it-yourself version, sit in the bathtub and run enough warm water to cover up to your navel. Fill a large bowl with cold water, place it in the bath and put your feet in it. Wrap a warm towel around your upper body and relax there for three minutes. Then drain the bath, refill it with cold water and sit in the water up to the navel. Fill a bowl with hot water and submerge the feet. Remain like this for one or two minutes and then take a warm shower.

salt glow

To enhance your circulation and deep-cleanse the body, treat yourself to a head-to-toe salt glow. Mix half a cup of coarse salt with a small amount of water to form a moist paste. Place a little of the mixture in each hand and work it over the skin, rubbing firmly to create friction to stimulate the body and skin. Start with your feet and work your way up the legs. Using the mixture as needed, work over the arms, back, abdomen, and chest (avoiding the delicate skin on your breasts and décolleté). Shower with warm water to rinse off and then vigorously rub over your skin with a towel. Go straight to bed after a salt glow and expect to sweat profusely. You can use a salt glow once a week if you have problems sweating, or once a month as part of a detoxing regimen.

water treatments

seaweed soak

Renowned for its deep-cleansing and healing properties, seaweed has been high on the list of natural remedies for centuries. To reap the benefits of a seaweed soak in the comfort of your own home, dilute 2 oz (60 g) of dried seaweed (available from health food stores) in a small amount of hot water. Allow the seaweed to dissolve, add it to a warm bath, and soak yourself in it for 20 minutes.

salty solution

For centuries, mineral-rich waters have provided a natural remedy to heal skin complaints, soothe aches and pains, and pep up circulation. People have long flocked to the Dead Sea to bathe in the waters to cure eczema and psoriasis. At home, sprinkle 2 cups of Dead Sea salts (available from health food stores) into the bath and soak in the tub for 20 minutes, adding more hot water when necessary.

liquid assets

hand bath

If you suffer from wrist strain and poor circulation, ease the symptoms with a hand bath. Fill a bowl with warm water, soak your hands for 3 minutes, then plunge into cold water for 30 seconds. Repeat three times. Adding a tablespoon of almond oil to the warm water will help condition the skin, or to improve circulation, run a powerful shower jet over your palms while in the bath.

water workout

Many health spas have specially made baths with powerful underwater jets that pummel you into shape while you relax. To do it yourself, immerse your body underwater and work over the body in circular motions with a shower head.

headache ease

To help soothe headaches, target the soles of the feet with a high-powered shower jet using cold water. Work over the underside of each foot in circular motions to stimulate the reflexology points, which in turn balance the activity of the body's major organs.

steamy solutions

The heat generated in steam rooms and saunas is designed to make you sweat profusely to assist with toxin excretion and help relieve congested sinuses. To create your own steam room, run the shower on the hottest setting for 10 minutes. Keep all the doors and windows closed. Undress and remain in the room for 10 minutes. Take a warm shower, scrub with an exfoliator, and finish with a cold shower. If you feel weak after a sauna, drink plenty of water and eat a banana to replace potassium lost from perspiring. Never use a sauna or steam room if you are pregnant, diabetic, epileptic, or suffer hypertension, asthma, heart disease, or respiratory problems.

treading water

If you're feel lethargic or your energy levels are flagging, run cold water in a bathtub until it reaches your calves and literally tread water for 5 minutes. Afterward you'll feel refreshed and energized. It's also a good way to help tone the lower legs.

play safe

ALWAYS TAKE a shower before getting into a hot tub. It will help prevent the spread of bacteria and impurities.

HOT TUBS ease aching muscles and joints, but they also raise blood pressure and heart rate and aren't advisable if you suffer from cardiovascular problems.

THE SUDDEN change in water temperatures used in hydrotherapy treatments can be a shock to the system and this type of treatment is not recommended if you suffer from a pulmonary condition.

SPEND ONLY 10 to 20 minutes in a hydrotherapy bath in order to reap the benefits without stressing the heart.

NEVER APPLY cold water to a chilled body. Warm up by taking a warm shower or exercising gently; then proceed with hydrotherapy treatments.

WHILE TAKING an Epsom salts bath, do not use soap; it can interfere with the activity of the salts.

NEVER HAVE more than two Epsom salts baths in a week.

restore

invigorate

energize

therapeutic baths

rebalance

rejuvenate

enliven

bath therapy

bathing benefits

Take to the bathtub to maintain your health. Bathing can help ward off minor ailments, treating everything from migraines to aching muscles.

medicinal baths

Very hot water (100ºF/38ºC) increases the activity of the sweat glands and is ideal if you want to get rid of a cold or flu. Stay in the bath for a maximum of 10 minutes and do not attempt this type of bath if you have heart problems or high blood pressure. Very cold baths (65–70ºF or 18–21ºC) are ideal for overcoming fatigue and poor circulation and improving muscle tone, and they are reputed to help relieve constipation. Stay in the bath for 3 to 5 minutes or for as long as you can tolerate it.

muscle fatigue

After strenuous physical activity, lactic acid builds up in the muscles, which leads to aches and pains. To relieve muscle fatigue, follow the ancient Japanese tradition of soaking in a rice vinegar bath. Add 2 cups (475 ml) of brown rice vinegar to a tepid bath and soak in it for 15 to 20 minutes.

insomnia

If you're having problems sleeping, try taking a warm bath scented with four drops of calming lavender essential oil before going to bed. Drink a glass of milk at bedtime — it enables the brain cells to absorb more tryptophan from the bloodstream. The brain then converts the tryptophan into a soothing chemical called serotonin, which induces a state of serenity.

bath remedies

swollen ankles

To reduce the swelling, use one drop each of cypress and lavender essential oils in a warm foot bath. Soak your feet for 10 minutes, then lie down with your feet raised on a couple of pillows, and drink plenty of water.

chilblains

To treat chilblains, pour boiling water into a large bowl and then leave until tepid. Add two drops each of lavender and black pepper essence to the water and soak your feet for 10 minutes. Afterward, dry your feet thoroughly. Rub neat tea tree oil on the affected parts to treat.

fluid retention

To help relieve fluid retention, add two drops of juniper oil and three of orange oil to the bath. A healthy diet rich in vitamin B, particularly B1, can help with fluid retention, and eating parsley, tarragon, leeks, and celery is beneficial. Try drinking a cup of nettle tea in the morning and early evening.

eczema/psoriasis

Try adding two drops of bergamot oil and three of lavender to the bath; take supplements of evening primrose oil; and massage wheat-germ oil on the affected areas of the body and face. If you have psoriasis on your scalp, before shampooing, massage the scalp with an infusion of marigold flowers. Steep four flower heads of English marigold (*Calendula officinalis*) in 2 cups (475 ml) of boiling water for 20 minutes, strain, and add the juice of half a lemon. Leave the infusion on the scalp for 3 to 4 minutes and shampoo as usual using a mild formula.

bath remedies

jet lag

Traveling through different time zones can throw your body rhythms out of synch. If you're taking a day flight or arrive at your destination in the morning, use one drop each of peppermint and eucalyptus oils to infuse the bath. If you're taking a night flight or arrive in the evening, take a warm bath with a drop each of lavender and chamomile. While flying, avoid eating airline food and stick to citrus fruits only. Step up your intake of mineral water to counteract the dry cabin air, and avoid alcohol, which only enhances dehydration.

sunburn

To take the sting out of sun-stressed skin, take a cool bath in which five drops of lavender or chamomile essential oils have been added. Soothe your sunburned skin by smoothing on calming aloe vera gel.

prickly heat

If you suffer from prickly heat, mix three drops each of lavender and eucalyptus essential oils in one tablespoon of jojoba oil and add this concoction to the bath water. You should also drink lots of mineral water.

bath remedies

colds

If you're suffering from a cold, opt for a mustard bath. It's a warming and stimulating remedy that also helps to improve circulation, boosts metabolism, and relieves fatigue, aches, and pains. Mix $1/2$ cup of powdered mustard with some cold water, add to a tepid bath, and relax in it for 10 to 15 minutes. If irritation occurs, stop bathing, and rinse off immediately. This type of bath is not recommended for children. After a mustard bath, pat the skin dry, wrap up warm, and go to bed.

menstrual pain

To help ease cramps, lace a warm bath with two drops of geranium oil and three of lavender. Lie down with a hot water bottle on your abdomen. Try to cut down on your intake of salt and caffeine. Eat foods rich in vitamin B6 such as meat, fish, and whole grains.

aching feet

For a pick-me-up for aching feet, fill a large bowl with warm water, add two drops of lemon or peppermint oil, and soak feet and ankles for 10 minutes.

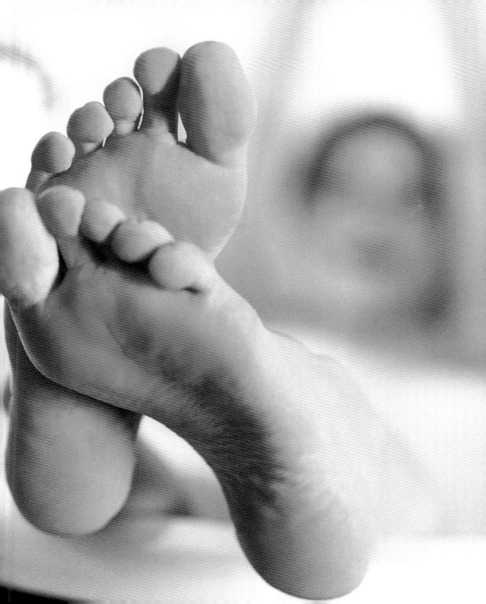

bath remedies

cystitis

If you suffer from cystitis, take a warm bath mixed with two drops each of sandalwood and lavender oils and one drop of eucalyptus oil. Try to drink at least 2 quarts of water a day to relieve the acidity of urine. You should also try drinking a glass of cranberry juice each day as a preventative measure.

migraine

To reduce the symptoms of migraine, blend four drops of lavender oil, two drops of marjoram, and two drops of rosemary oils with 2 oz (60 ml) of jojoba oil and store in a dark glass bottle. When a migraine starts, pour a small amount of the blend into the bath. While you're soaking, place a hot cloth over your forehead, and then close your eyes. Relax your breathing, inhaling deeply through the nose, and exhaling through the mouth.

backache

To help soothe a stiff back, add three drops of lavender oil and two drops of marjoram to a bath and relax for 10 to 15 minutes. To remove tension from back muscles, sit on a chair and tense your muscles by pushing your lower back hard against the back of the chair. Relax and repeat several times.

bad circulation

Pep up bad circulation with a stimulating bath blend of cypress, neroli, lemon, and rose oils. Exercise regularly (try a brisk walk or bike ride), have professional massages, and practice dry skin brushing. Avoid coffee, tea, and alcohol, and try making tisanes from parsley and sage. Increase your intake of foods rich in vitamins C and E and bioflavonoids. Onions, garlic, citrus fruits, and wheat germ will help boost sluggish circulation.

relax

unwind

retreat

bathing solutions

recharge

revive

escape

bathing tips

exfoliating treat

Treat neglected skin to an intensive double-strength exfoliating experience. First, massage a scrub into the damp skin, working in small circular motions, then shower off, and buff over the body with a mitt or loofah.

bathtime

The natural oils in the skin keep bacteria out and moisture in. Having more than two baths or showers in a day will strip the skin of this protective barrier.

body scrub

If you're out of exfoliator, use a handful of coarse sea salt or oatmeal instead.

moisture boost

For a postbath skin fix, slather on a moisturizing preparation while your skin is slightly damp. For boosting very dry skin, smooth on a nourishing oil, such as sweet almond oil, and seal in by applying a rich body moisturizer.

soap alternative

If you are allergic to soap, herbal practitioners recommend the use of a muslin or gauze bag filled with a tablespoon of dried chamomile flowers, lavender, and rose petals to gently cleanse and exfoliate the skin. Work over the skin, then leave the bag in the bathtub to scent the water.

bathing tips

compress work

Aromatic compresses can help improve your state of mind when you're in the bath. Dip a face cloth into a bowl of warm water infused with 1 or 2 drops of your chosen essential oil, wring out the cloth, press it into your face, and inhale deeply. To calm an overactive mind, use orange essential oil; to relieve tension, try chamomile oil; to boost your confidence, opt for neroli; and to improve your concentration and mental performance, use rosemary oil.

musical notes

To induce peace and tranquillity, listen to Handel's *Water Music* or tune into the soothing sounds of whales, dolphins, Gregorian chants, or the sea.

bath additives

You do not need to splurge on fancy bath and body preparations. You can invest in basic, unscented preparations and then lace them with your favorite fragrance or add a couple of drops of essential oils.

bathing tips

winter warmer

To take the chill out of cold winter nights, grate a 3/4 in (2 cm) cube of root ginger and place in a piece of muslin, tie with string, and then throw in the tub while the water is running. Ginger is reputed to boost circulation and has a warming effect on the senses.

sock it

Those who have overactive minds and problems sleeping will benefit from this hydrotherapy treatment. Soak a pair of cotton socks in cold water, wring out, and put them on. Cover with a dry pair of wool or cotton socks and go to bed. The temperature of the damp socks will draw energy from your body, making you feel calm and relaxed.

foot scrub

If you don't have a pumice stone on hand, you can use an avocado pit instead to remove calluses and stubborn, tough skin on the feet. It's a natural abrasive that can be enriched with a few drops of eucalyptus oil to help deodorize and scent the feet.

milk bath

Cleopatra and Mary, Queen of Scots bathed in milk because it contains proteins, which soften skin, and lactic acid, which helps dissolve superfluous skin cells. Add 2 cups (475 ml) of milk to a warm bath with a drop of jasmine oil for a pleasant smell.

mud masks

For a deep cleansing treat, slather on a mud or clay body mask before getting in the bath. These literally vacuum clean the skin — they contain negatively charged ions that attract positively charged impurities. For best results, sponge onto damp skin, leave for the required time, and shower before soaking in an aromatic bath. The main therapeutic ingredient found in mud and clay masks is magnesium, which acts on the nervous and lymphatic systems, so these products are not merely skin-deep. Use them as part of a detoxing regime, for alleviating chronic ailments such as rheumatism, arthritis, acne, eczema, and psoriasis, and for their beautifying benefits.